Book B

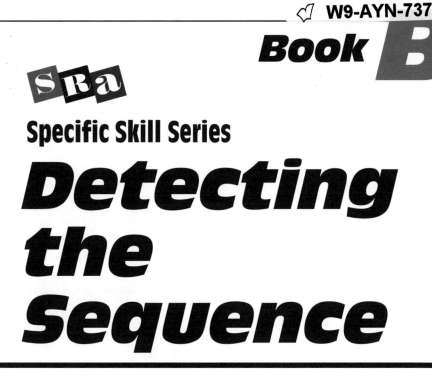

Specific Skill Series

Detecting the Sequence

Richard A. Boning

Fifth Edition

SRA/McGraw-Hill

Columbus, Ohio

Cover, Back Cover, Wayne Lynch/Masterfile

SRA/McGraw-Hill

A Division of The **McGraw·Hill** Companies

Printed in the United States of America.

Send all inquiries to:
SRA/McGraw-Hill
8787 Orion Place
Columbus, OH 43240-4027

ISBN 0-02-687992-1

6 7 8 IPC 02 01 00

PURPOSE:

DETECTING THE SEQUENCE helps develop the important ability to determine time relationships—the order in which things happen. Proficiency in this often taken-for-granted skill is necessary in all kinds of academic and nonacademic reading, from narration to process explanation.

FOR WHOM:

The skill of DETECTING THE SEQUENCE is developed through a series of books spanning ten levels (Picture, Preparatory, A, B, C, D, E, F, G, H). The Picture Level is for pupils who have not acquired a basic sight vocabulary. The Preparatory Level is for pupils who have a basic sight vocabulary but are not yet ready for the first-grade-level book. Books A through H are appropriate for pupils who can read on levels one through eight, respectively. **The use of the *Specific Skill Series Placement Test* is recommended to determine the appropriate level.**

THE NEW EDITION:

DETECTING THE SEQUENCE has been designed to help improve students' skills in identifying the sequence of events within a reading selection. In this series, the variety of questions helps develop students' understanding of multiple ways of expressing time relationships. Questions are text-dependent rather than picture-dependent.

SESSIONS:

Short practice sessions are the most effective. It is desirable to have a practice session every day or every other day, using a few units each session.

To the Teacher

SCORING:

Pupils should record their answers on the reproducible worksheets. The worksheets make scoring easier and provide uniform records of the pupils' work. Using worksheets also avoids consuming the exercise books.

It is important for pupils to know how well they are doing. For this reason, units should be scored as soon as they have been completed. Then a discussion can be held in which pupils justify their choices. (The Integrated Language Activities, many of which are open-ended, do not lend themselves to an objective score; thus there are no answer keys for these pages.)

GENERAL INFORMATION ON *DETECTING THE SEQUENCE*:

DETECTING THE SEQUENCE helps develop sequence skills through three general types of questions: (1) those that focus directly on when an event happened; (2) those that focus on which of several events happened first (or last) among the events mentioned; and (3) those that focus on whether a particular event happened before, at the same time as, or after another. The teacher should make clear to students that a question reading "Which happened first (last)?" means "Which happened before (after) any of the *other answer choices*?" (not "Which happened first [last] in the entire reading selection?").

Answering questions in DETECTING THE SEQUENCE involves more than just reading for facts. Most questions require pupils to establish the time relationships between two separately stated ideas by utilizing time clues in the text. (On the Picture Level, pupils examine two pictures illustrating a sequence of events, and determine which event happened first.)

SUGGESTED STEPS:

On all levels above Picture, pupils should read each story carefully. At the end of each statement they should try to form a picture in their minds so that they will clearly understand what happened first, second, and so forth. As they read, pupils should look for key words that serve as sequence clues, such as *then*, *before*, *soon*, *finally*, *later*, *while*, *when*, and *now*. After finishing the story, pupils should review it mentally. Without looking at the story, they should be able to recall the sequence in which events occurred. If they cannot do this, they should reread the story. Pupils should then answer the questions on their worksheets. In answering, pupils may look at the story as often as necessary.

RELATED MATERIALS:

Specific Skill Series Placement Tests, which enable the teacher to place pupils at their appropriate levels in each skill, are available for the Elementary (Pre-1–6) and Midway (4–8) grade levels.

About This Book

In real life, things happen in a certain order. First one thing happens, then another. When you read a story, it is often told in order, too. Things that happened first are told first. This story tells things in order.

Dan wanted a pet. He went to the pet store. Dan got a black and white cat.

Sometimes the order is turned around. Read this sentence.

Before Dan went to school, he fed the cat.

Which happened first: *Dan went to school* or *Dan fed the cat*? You can tell that Dan fed the cat first. The word *before* tells you. Words like *after*, *before*, *then*, *next*, *first*, and *last* are all clues. They let you know the order of the things that happened.

Often one thing must happen before another thing can happen. You must get on your bike before you can ride it. You can't read a book until after you have opened it. You know what happens first because it would not make sense for things to happen the other way around.

In this book, you will read short stories. As you read each story, think about what happened first, next, and last. Then answer two questions about the story. Each question asks you about the order in which things happened.

Have you ever lost a balloon? Did you wonder where it went or how far it could fly? Some children at a school in Dobbs Ferry, New York, tried to find out.

On a windy day, the children let a lot of balloons go. First, they wrote their names on cards. They also wrote where they went to school. Then they tied the cards to the balloons. They hoped the people who found the balloons would write back to them. Finally, the children let the balloons go. Off the balloons flew, high into the sky.

The children waited to hear news about their balloons. They wanted to know how far each balloon went. They wanted to know who had found it. One month later, they got a letter from a sheep farmer far away in Australia. He had found one of the balloons. It had traveled 10,000 miles! No one thought a balloon could go so far!

---

1. **Which of these things happened first?**

   (A) The children let the balloons go.

   (B) They tied the cards to the balloons.

   (C) The children wrote their names on cards.

2. **What happened after the children let the balloons go?**

   (A) On cards, they wrote where they went to school.

   (B) They got a letter from a farmer in Australia.

   (C) They tied the cards to the balloons.

UNIT 2
Balto, the Life Saver

In 1925, a dog named Balto saved people's lives. People who lived in Nome, Alaska, were very sick. The doctors in Nome could not help them.

Doctors 800 miles away had medicine that could help. It was winter, though, and the snow was deep. The only way to get through the snow was with sleds pulled by dogs. In those days, one team of dogs could not go all the way to Nome. Different teams of dogs lived along the way. So each team went only part of the way. Then another team of dogs took over.

A storm had started by the time it was Balto's turn. The snow was very thick. People could not see, but Balto and his team did not get lost. Almost a day after Balto's team started, the sled got to Nome. It was late. People were very worried. But when they saw Balto, they cheered. The medicine that Balto brought saved many lives in Nome.

---

1. **Which of these things happened last?**

   (A) A bad snow storm started.

   (B) Medicine saved many lives in Nome.

   (C) Balto got to Nome in about a day.

2. **What was going on while Balto was trying to get to Nome?**

   (A) It was snowing hard.

   (B) People in Nome were cheering.

   (C) Many lives were being saved.

In the fall, what can you do with a pile of leaves? One thing you can do is make a leaf print. Look through the pile for a large leaf that is not ripped.

To make a leaf print, you first take the large leaf and dry it well. Then pour some colored paint into a pie pan. Next, roll a roller in the paint. After that, roll the roller on one side of the leaf.

When the leaf is covered with paint, press it onto a sheet of paper. Press straight down. Try not to push the leaf across the paper even a little bit. Finally, lift the leaf off the paper. Be careful when you lift up the leaf. You must lift it straight up.

Now look at your leaf print. What do you see? Does it look just like the leaf?

---

1. **Which of these things do you do first?**

    (A) Dry the leaf well.

    (B) Roll paint on the leaf.

    (C) Press the leaf onto some paper.

2. **What do you do before you roll the roller onto the leaf?**

    (A) Be careful when you lift up the leaf.

    (B) Press straight down.

    (C) Roll a roller in the paint.

UNIT 4
A Ship out of Water

A hotel is a place where people stay when they go on a trip. A ship once became a hotel far from the water. How did this happen?

The ship was on the ocean near South America. All at once, a giant wave came toward the ship. The wave was more than 50 feet high! Everyone held on tightly as the wave hit the ship.

The ship rode on top of the giant wave. On and on it went. At last, the ship stopped. Then the wave pulled back, leaving the ship behind. After that, the people on the ship went to sleep. They didn't know where they were.

The next morning, the people saw that they were far from the water. The ship was only 200 feet from some tall mountains! There was no way to get it back to the ocean.

Since the ship could not be a ship anymore, it was sold. For a while, it was a hotel. Later, it became a hospital.

---

1. **Which of these things happened last?**

   (A) The people went to sleep.

   (B) A giant wave hit the ship.

   (C) The ship became a hotel.

2. **What happened before the giant wave hit the ship?**

   (A) The ship was on the ocean.

   (B) The ship was sold.

   (C) At last, the ship stopped.

UNIT 5
A Crow Named Hello

Mr. Green knows a lot about animals. He often takes care of wild animals that are too young to care for themselves. One day, Mr. Green's friend brought a baby crow to him. The crow had fallen out of its nest. The friend knew that Mr. Green would take care of the baby crow.

Mr. Green called the bird Hello. At first, Hello just hopped around. It flapped its wings, but it could not fly yet. It liked to pick things up in its mouth and throw them down.

When Hello learned to fly, it would fly up into a tree. Then it would open its mouth and cry. The crow wanted someone to bring food to it! No one did that, of course. Finally, Hello would come down out of the tree to get food.

At last, Hello was all grown up. One day, Hello ate its food and flew off again. It never came back.

---

1. **Which of these things happened first?**

   (A) Mr. Green's friend brought a baby crow to him.

   (B) The baby crow fell out of its nest.

   (C) Mr. Green named the crow Hello.

2. **What did the crow do after it grew up?**

   (A) It just hopped around.

   (B) It opened its mouth and cried.

   (C) It flew away and never came back.

UNIT 6
The Day It Rained Money

Sometimes people wish it would rain money. They wish money would fall on the ground all around them so that they could just pick it up. One day in Ohio, that is what happened! A bank truck was driving along, full of money. All of a sudden, its back door swung open! Bags of money fell out and hit the road.

Next, cars ran into the bags of money. This made the bags break. Money flew up into the air! One person said the road "was just full of money."

Soon, money was all over the road. People stopped their cars. Then they got out and started to pick up all the money. Most people took the money to the police. One man turned in $57,670! In the end, the police gave the money back to the bank.

---

1. **Which of these things happened last?**

   (A) The police gave the money back to the bank.

   (B) People stopped and picked up the money.

   (C) The road was full of money.

2. **What happened before the money bags fell into the road?**

   (A) Cars hit the bags of money.

   (B) Money flew up into the air.

   (C) The back door of the truck swung open.

UNIT 7
A Race with Fire

A lot of smoke hid the sun. Everything was black. The ground was so hot it burned the feet. The people who were fighting the fire looked at what had already burned. Then they thought about what they could do next.

All of a sudden, the wind changed! The fire started to come toward the people! "Hop on!" cried Pixie Vogt, one of the people there to fight the fire. She quickly started up her fire truck. Before she could get going, the fire jumped across the road! Three men were burned, but they got on the truck. "Let's get going!" Pixie shouted.

It was a race with the fire. Which could go faster, the fire or Pixie's truck? Faster and faster she drove, with the fire close behind. The other people held on tightly to the truck. No one wanted to be left behind!

At last, Pixie beat the fire. The flames were far behind the racing truck. They were all safe!

---

1. **Which of these things happened first?**

   (A) Three men were burned, but they got on the truck.

   (B) The wind changed, and the fire came toward the people.

   (C) Pixie shouted, "Let's get going!"

2. **What happened before Pixie could get the fire truck going?**

   (A) The truck raced against the fire.

   (B) The fire jumped across the road.

   (C) Pixie beat the fire.

UNIT 8
Space Monkeys

Before people went into space, animals did. The very first chimp (a kind of monkey) to go up into space was named Ham. Ham went 156 miles above the earth. Ham flew for only 16 minutes. The spaceship landed in the ocean, and Ham was not hurt.

The second chimp in space was named Enos. Enos was the first chimp to go around the earth in a spaceship. The trip lasted over 3 hours!

While Enos was flying around the earth, he had work to do. He could eat and drink during his trip too.

After his trip, Enos landed in the ocean. Then a boat picked up his spaceship. When the spaceship was opened, Enos hopped out. First, Enos just took a breath of fresh air. Then he shook hands with all the people on the boat! Everyone could tell that Enos was happy to be back on Earth!

---

1. **What was the last thing to happen to Enos?**

    (A) Enos hopped out of his spaceship.

    (B) Enos shook hands with the people on the boat.

    (C) Enos landed in the ocean.

2. **What happened while Enos was going around the earth?**

    (A) He ate, drank, and did some work.

    (B) His spaceship landed in the ocean.

    (C) Enos shook hands with the people on the boat.

Sometimes a pet can be your friend when you have no one to play with. Sometimes a stuffed animal or a doll can be a friend. Even a ball or a jump rope can make you feel less lonely when you want to play. But have you ever thought that a leaf could be your friend?

One cold, windy day, Brenda walked to the playground. It was empty. She sat on a swing and looked all around. There was no one to play with. Then Brenda looked at a tree nearby. The tree had one leaf left on it. Then the wind blew the leaf off the tree. The leaf danced in the wind. It flew around Brenda's head. "Come play with me," the leaf seemed to say.

Brenda ran after the leaf. She chased it around the playground. The leaf always stayed ahead of her. Finally, it blew onto the ground. Brenda picked up the leaf. She put it under the tree. "Thank you for playing with me," she said. Then she went home for lunch.

---

1. **What happened first?**

    (A) Brenda sat on a swing.

    (B) The wind blew a leaf off a tree.

    (C) Brenda walked to the playground.

2. **What happened right after the leaf blew onto the ground?**

    (A) The leaf danced in the wind.

    (B) Brenda picked up the leaf.

    (C) Brenda chased the leaf.

UNIT 10
A Long Fall

One day, a man was flying a jet plane 47,000 feet in the air. Below the plane was a big storm. All of a sudden, the plane stopped going! Then it started to fall! The man knew he had to get out of the plane! He jumped with a parachute. A parachute is like a balloon that lets you fall slowly through the air.

Down and down he fell! The air was very cold. As he fell, he looked at his watch. It said 6:05.

At 10,000 feet, the man's parachute opened. He felt safe then, but he had fallen right into the storm! He said he was "in an angry ocean of clouds." Then the wind hit him. It sent him flying up and up again. The wind threw him all over. Sometimes he went up. Sometimes he went to the side. It was raining very hard.

At last, the man passed through the storm. Finally, he landed on the ground. When he looked at his watch, it read 6:40. He had been tossed around in the air for more than half an hour!

---

1. **Which of these things happened last?**

   (A) The man fell into the angry ocean of clouds.

   (B) The man landed on the ground.

   (C) The man saw that his watch read 6:40.

2. **What happened before the man left the plane?**

   (A) He saw that his watch read 6:05.

   (B) The plane stopped and began to fall.

   (C) The man was tossed around in the air.

Elsa hoped to be an artist when she grew up. She decided she would paint one picture every day. On Friday, she carried her paint box outside. She had decided to make her picture outdoors. What could she paint? Elsa looked around. She had already painted pictures of the houses and trees. It was time to paint something new. Then Elsa looked at the sky. The sun was sinking. The clouds were pink, blue, and purple. She would paint the sky!

Before Elsa picked up her brush, she spread out a piece of paper. Next, she dipped her brush into the red paint. She painted a beautiful red sun. Then she painted the bright clouds. As she watched, the sky kept changing. Elsa tried to make the colors in her picture look like the colors in the sky. Finally, Elsa looked at her picture. It was almost as beautiful as the real sky.

---

1. **Which of these things happened first?**

    (A) Elsa looked at the houses and trees.

    (B) Elsa carried her paint box outside.

    (C) Elsa looked at the sky.

2. **What did Elsa do right before she picked up her brush?**

    (A) She watched the sky changing.

    (B) She looked at her picture.

    (C) She spread out a piece of paper.

UNIT 12
Johnny Appleseed

Do you like to eat apples? Have you ever thought of planting an apple tree? Then you could grow your own apples to eat. That is what John Chapman did long ago.

Even when he was very little, John Chapman loved apples. When he was grown, he still loved apples. So he grew apple trees to sell. Soon he began giving apple trees away to people going west. Then one day, he went west himself.

Everywhere he went, John planted apple trees. He would stop at a town. Then he would get people to help him clear some land. Next, he would plant apple seeds. After the trees were growing well, John would move on. He would do this all over again in the next place he came to.

For fifty years, John Chapman went from place to place. Sometimes he returned to places he had been before. Then he could visit old friends and see the apple trees he had helped to plant. After a while, people forgot what his real name was. They called him Johnny Appleseed.

---

1. **Which of these things happened last?**

    (A) Everywhere he went, John planted apple trees.

    (B) John decided to go west himself.

    (C) John gave apple trees away to people going west.

2. **When John stopped at a town, what did he do first?**

    (A) He planted apple seeds.

    (B) He got people to help him clear land.

    (C) He waited for the apple trees to grow.

When Hello learned to fly, it would fly up into a tree. Then it would open its mouth and cry. The crow wanted someone to bring food to it!

A. Exercising Your Skill

The part of a story above tells about some things that a crow named Hello did. The words *when* and *then* help you know when Hello did things. These are called time-order words. Think of some other time-order words like *first* and *next*. On your paper, copy the heading and the list. Then add other time-order words.

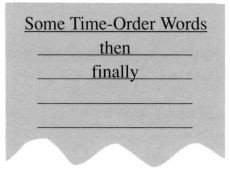

Some Time-Order Words
then
finally
_____
_____

B. Expanding Your Skill

Talk with a classmate about the time-order words you wrote on your paper. If you think of any more words, add them to your list.

Think about things you do that take only one step, like writing your first name. Think of things that take more than one step, like writing a heading on your paper. On your paper, write the things in the box that take **more than** one step to do.

getting dressed	eating breakfast
checking the time	getting to school
playing a game	doing a math problem

C. Exploring Language

In each story below, the sentences are in the wrong order. Choose one story. Write it on your paper. Put the sentences in the **right** order. Then write an ending.

1. Yori put his painting on the wall. Yori painted a picture of his dog. Yori got some paints for his birthday.

   Ending: _____

2. Jill got on the school bus. Jill went to the bus stop. Jill waited for the school bus. Jill sat in the seat next to Lora.

   Ending: _____

3. Tina started to build a snow house. Tina went outside in the snow. They worked on the snow house together. Tina's dad came out to help build it.

   Ending: _____

D. Expressing Yourself

Do one of these things.

1. Play a mixed-up story game. Choose three parts from a story like "Jack and the Beanstalk" or "Hansel and Gretel." Tell the parts out of order. See if your classmates can put them in the right order.

2. Draw a set of four pictures that show something happening in order—first, second, third, and last. Mix up the pictures and give them to a classmate. See if he or she can put them in the right order and tell what is happening in each picture.

UNIT 13
Life on the Plains

What do you think it was like for people to go west over 100 years ago? Many families left their homes in the East at that time. They moved to flat, grassy places in the middle of the United States and Canada called the plains.

Most of the people who moved to the plains were farmers. When they got to the plains, they found problems. There were very few trees on the plains. The farmers needed wood from trees to build houses. Also, the flat, grassy land had bunches of heavy roots just below it. It would be very hard to get that kind of dirt ready for farming.

The farmers didn't give up, though. First, they cut up the earth, roots and all, into blocks. They used these blocks of earth and roots to build strong houses. Then they began the hard work of breaking up the rest of the land for farming. It took a long time, but they did it. Most of the farms in the United States and Canada today are on the plains.

---

1. **Which of these things happened first?**

   (A) Farmers cut the earth into blocks.

   (B) Farmers built strong houses.

   (C) Farmers moved to the plains.

2. **What did farmers do after they had built their houses?**

   (A) They cut the earth into blocks.

   (B) They left their homes in the East.

   (C) They broke up the rest of the land for farming.

UNIT 14
Floating Soap

Most soap bars sink when you put them in water. But there is one kind of soap that floats. About a hundred years ago, this soap was no different from other soaps. It sank, too. How did this soap become different from other soaps?

One day, a worker in the soap factory went to lunch. He forgot to turn off his machine. While he was gone, the machine kept working. It didn't just mix the soap. It beat air into the soap!

One man in the soap factory decided to see what this new soap would be like. He found that the soap floated in water! The owner of the factory thought that people might like a soap bar that floated. It would be easy to find in the tub if you let go of it! That was how this soap came to be different from other soaps.

---

1. **Which of these things happened last?**

   (A) The machine beat air into the soap.

   (B) The worker forgot to turn off his machine.

   (C) A worker went to lunch.

2. **What happened after the man decided to try the new soap?**

   (A) All soaps sank in water.

   (B) He found that the soap floated.

   (C) The machine beat air into the soap.

UNIT 15
Mount St. Helens

Mount St. Helens is a large volcano in Washington. Before May 18, 1980, Mount St. Helens was over 9,000 feet high. After May 18, the mountain was only 8,364 feet high. What happened on that day? Mount St. Helens blew its top off!

First, the ground began to shake. Then the top of the mountain broke open. Next, hot air blasted out of the opening. The air moved so fast that it knocked down trees 17 miles away! At the same time, hot ash and broken rocks blew into the sky.

The terrific heat started forest fires around the mountain. Melted rock poured down the mountain. It covered buildings and bridges and filled in rivers.

By the end of the day, everything around Mount St. Helens was gone. Lakes and streams were buried. Trees and other plants were blown down or burned. Birds, fish, animals, and even people, died. Nothing was the same as it had been before May 18, 1980.

---

1. **Which of these things happened first?**

    (A) The top of the mountain broke open.

    (B) Rocks flew into the air.

    (C) The ground began to shake.

2. **What happened after hot air came out of the mountain?**

    (A) The top of the mountain broke open.

    (B) Mount St. Helens was over 9,000 feet high.

    (C) Trees were knocked down 17 miles away.

The first woman to fly across the Atlantic Ocean was Amelia Earhart. That was a brave thing to do, but Amelia was not easily scared—not even as a child.

Growing up, Amelia loved to play games like baseball and basketball. She and her sister Muriel used to play long and hard every day.

Amelia also loved going to school. She liked reading many books and learning new things.

When Amelia was in the third grade, her mother and father took her to a state fair. There she saw her first airplane. She decided then that she wanted to learn to fly.

It was many years before Amelia Earhart was old enough to begin flying. Once she began, though, she made up for lost time! She flew very fast and very far. After she flew across the Atlantic Ocean, she wrote a book about it. The President even invited her to the White House and said he was proud of her.

---

1. **Which of these things happened last?**

   (A) Amelia played with her sister.

   (B) Amelia wrote a book.

   (C) Amelia started to fly.

2. **Which of these things happened before Amelia Earhart flew across the Atlantic Ocean?**

   (A) She visited the White House.

   (B) She wrote a book.

   (C) She went to a state fair.

Long ago, the Plains Indians were hunters. They didn't live in one place. They followed the animals that they hunted. Since they had to move often and quickly, they lived in houses called tipis (say "TEE peez"). These houses looked like pointed tents.

To make a tipi, the people first cut long, straight poles. A large tipi might use twenty-five poles! Then the people set the poles up in a circle on the ground. All the poles leaned in. The tops of the poles came together. Next, the people put animal hides together over the poles. The hides covered all the spaces between the poles. Sometimes people painted pictures on the hides. They left a flap for a door at one side. They left the top open to let smoke out.

When the people wanted to move, they just folded up the tipis. At first, dogs pulled the tipi poles along to the next place. Later, horses did the work.

---

1. **Which of these things happened first?**

    (A) Horses pulled the tipi poles from place to place.

    (B) The people folded up the tipis.

    (C) Dogs pulled the tipi poles.

2. **What did the people do before they put the hides together?**

    (A) They set the tipi poles up in a circle.

    (B) They left a flap for a door.

    (C) They folded up the tipis.

UNIT 18
Birds and Weddings

When people get married, their friends often throw rice at them. This is supposed to be good luck. It isn't good luck for birds, though. Birds eat the rice. Rice that has not been cooked can make birds sick.

After some people learned that rice is bad for birds, they wanted to change things. They did not want birds to become sick because of the rice. They came up with a good idea. First they put bird seed in pretty little bags. Then they sold the bags of bird seed to people going to weddings. The people threw the bird seed instead of rice. The birds had a good meal!

Long ago, people did not throw rice at people who were just married. People started throwing rice just over 100 years ago. Before that, friends of people getting married threw corn at them. Guess what? Corn is often used to make bird seed!

---

1. **Which of these things happened last?**

    (A) The people put bird seed in little bags.

    (B) The birds ate the bird seed thrown at weddings.

    (C) Friends threw rice at the people getting married.

2. **What happened just after friends threw rice?**

    (A) Birds ate the rice and got sick.

    (B) The people got married.

    (C) The birds had a good meal.

A space shuttle sat still in the cool morning air. It pointed up toward the bright blue sky. Many people had come to see it take off. Many more people were watching it on TV. Five men and women were in the spaceship waiting. Soon they would be looking back at the earth from far away. "Count down, ten seconds," said the voice. "Nine, eight, seven, six, five, four, three, two, one!" At first, there was just a low sound. Then the sound became a loud roar! Next, fire and smoke spilled out from the bottom of the shuttle! For a short time, it seemed not to move. Then slowly, slowly, it moved up and up on a tail of fire!

Up and up the shuttle went. It left huge clouds of fire and smoke behind it. Then it became smaller and smaller. After a while, the shuttle was only a bright light far up in the sky. Then it was gone.

---

1. **Which of these things happened first?**

    (A) Fire and smoke came from the bottom of the spaceship.

    (B) A low sound came from the ship.

    (C) A voice counted down from ten.

2. **What happened while the ship was going up?**

    (A) It left fire and smoke behind.

    (B) It sat still in the cool morning air.

    (C) The sound became a loud roar.

Lucy wanted to surprise her mom and dad. She decided to make a special lunch for them. She waited until they left the house one day. Then she got out things to make an egg and cheese pie.

First, she got out a pie pan. Then she beat three eggs with some milk in a bowl. She cut up some cheese into small pieces and put the pieces into the bowl. Finally, she poured everything into the pie pan and baked it. While the pie was baking, she cut up some fresh fruit and put it into a big bowl.

When Lucy's mom and dad came home, the house smelled good. The pie was a wonderful surprise! Everyone ate cheese pie and fruit for lunch. Lucy's mom and dad said it was the best lunch ever.

---

1. **Which of these things happened last?**

   (A) Lucy got out a pie pan.

   (B) Lucy's mom and dad left the house.

   (C) The house smelled good.

2. **What did Lucy do before she cut up the cheese?**

   (A) She poured everything into the pan.

   (B) She beat three eggs with some milk.

   (C) She baked the pie.

You do not need to buy a drum set to play the drums. There are many ways to make a drum. You can use an empty box. You can turn a big bowl or pan upside down. You can beat your drum with your hand or with a stick or with a spoon. In some parts of Africa, girls who live along rivers and lakes play water drums. They do not even need to make a drum. The drum is the river or lake!

First, the girl goes into the river up to her waist, or middle. Next, she cups each hand in the shape of a spoon. Then she beats the water with her hands. To make different sounds, she hits the water in different places and in different ways. Sometimes she hits it near the top. Then she pushes her hand down deeper.

While the girls play their water drums, they sing. Their mothers teach them some of the songs. They may also sing songs they hear on the radio. The songs that are the most fun are the ones they make up themselves!

---

1. **Which of these things happens first?**

   (A) The girl beats the water with her hands.

   (B) The girl cups her hands into the shape of spoons.

   (C) The girl goes into the water.

2. **What do the girls do while they are playing the water drums?**

   (A) They listen to songs on the radio.

   (B) They sing songs.

   (C) They beat their drums with a spoon.

UNIT 22
Step Gardens

If you lived on the side of a mountain, how would you grow food to eat? Some people in South America called the Incas (say "ING kuz") had just that problem hundreds of years ago.

Before they could plant seeds, the Incas had to make some flat land. They dug into the side of the mountain and made flat places that looked like big steps. Each step was a small field or garden. They built low stone walls to keep the dirt in place. Then they built smaller steps up the mountain. The Inca farmers climbed up and down these steps to get from one field to another.

Finally, the Incas could plant their seeds. They grew corn, potatoes, and beans in their step gardens. This gave them enough food to feed all their people. Their step gardens were made so well that many are still there today.

---

1. **Which of these things happened last?**

    (A) The Incas made stone walls.

    (B) The Incas planted seeds.

    (C) The Incas made some flat land.

2. **Which of these things happened before the stone walls were built?**

    (A) The Incas dug into the side of the mountains.

    (B) The Incas planted their seeds.

    (C) Potatoes, corn, and beans grew.

In 1918, the U.S. Post Office first tried using an airplane to carry the mail. Airmail did not get off to a good start, though.

First, the plane would not go. The workers couldn't find out what was wrong. Finally, someone looked to see if there was enough gas in the plane. There was no gas!

After the plane was filled with gas, the pilot (the person who flies the plane) took off. Once he was in the air, he started to follow some train tracks on the ground. He thought they went the right way. He was wrong! When he saw he was lost, he decided to land the plane. He wanted to ask someone which way he should go.

When he tried to land, the pilot broke part of the plane. It couldn't take off again. In the end, the mail had to be sent by truck!

---

1. **Which of these things happened first?**

   (A) The plane was filled with gas.

   (B) The plane would not go.

   (C) The plane took off into the air.

2. **What happened before the pilot decided to land the plane?**

   (A) The pilot broke part of the plane.

   (B) The mail had to be sent by truck.

   (C) The pilot followed the wrong train tracks.

UNIT 24
Time to Move

Some birds fly south for the winter. In the spring, they fly back north. Some people move with the seasons (parts of the year) too.

In the Alps, which are big mountains, winters are very cold. There is a lot of snow. While the snow is deep, the people stay in their warm houses. They keep their cows, goats, and sheep in barns. During the winter, the animals eat grass that was cut in the summer. When spring comes, everyone is ready to go outside!

After the snow melts, the mountains become covered with grass. Then it is time to move. The farmers take their animals up the mountain for the summer. They both will stay there until fall. They will cut long grass and store it for the winter. After the summer is over, the farmers and their animals will go back down the mountain again.

---

1. **Which of these things happens last?**

    (A) The mountains become covered with grass.

    (B) The farmers take their animals up the mountain.

    (C) The snow melts.

2. **What happens while the snow is deep?**

    (A) The farmers cut long grass.

    (B) The farmers keep their animals in barns.

    (C) The farmers take their animals up the mountain.

A tipi is a home made of animal hides. To make a tipi, the people *first* cut long, straight poles. A large tipi might use twenty-five poles! *Then* the people set the poles up in a circle on the ground. All the poles leaned in. The tops of the poles came together. *Next*, the people put animal hides together over the poles. They left a flap for a door at one side. They left the top open to let smoke out.

A. Exercising Your Skill

The story above tells how people made tipis. The steps are given in order. The steps have time-order words such as *first*, *then*, and *next*. Steps that tell how to do something or how to make something are called **directions**.

Think about directions you have seen or heard lately. Has your teacher given you any directions? Did you read directions to put a toy together? On your paper, write the names of two kinds of directions you have seen or heard lately. For example, one kind might be *Making a Kite*.

B. Expanding Your Skill

Talk with a classmate about the kinds of directions you wrote. If you think of other kinds, add them to your list.

Now pick one kind of direction from your list. Tell your classmate the steps of the directions, in the right order. Ask him or her if your steps are easy to understand. Then listen to your classmate's directions. Do you think the steps are in the right order?

C. Exploring Language

The following sets of directions are out of order. Think of the right order for the steps. Then write the underlined part of each step in order on your paper. Add time-order words like *first*, *next*, *then*, *last*.

1. How to Plant Flower Seeds
   - <u>Poke holes</u> in the dirt for the seeds.
   - <u>Pat the dirt</u>.
   - <u>Cover the seeds</u> with a little dirt.
   - <u>Drop the seeds</u> in the holes.

2. How To Build a Log Cabin
   - <u>Cut trees</u> to make logs.
   - <u>Lay down four logs</u> in a square shape on the ground.
   - <u>Put some logs across the top</u> for the roof.
   - <u>Add a row of four logs</u> to the first four logs.

D. Expressing Yourself

Do one of these things.

1. Make up a treasure hunt game. Hide the "treasure." Write clues on slips of paper. Each clue should give a step for finding the treasure. Ask one person to follow the clues to find the treasure.

2. With a partner, write a set of directions for someone to follow in your classroom. For example, the directions might say, "Walk to the end of row one. Shake hands with the last person in that row. Ask that person to follow you to the front of the room. Return to your seat." Have another classmate follow your directions.

Molly wanted to play a trick on her friends. First she said, "I can pour water into just one glass but fill up ten glasses at the same time!"

Then Molly set up the glasses in a special way. First, she put six glasses in a circle. Then she made a middle ring on top of them with three more glasses. She put the last glass on top of the three glasses. At last, she was ready to start the trick.

Molly took a bottle and began pouring water into the top glass. When the glass was full, water poured over the edge. Molly kept on pouring. The water went into the three glasses in the middle ring. After they were full, the water poured over their edges. Molly kept right on pouring. This time, the water went into the six glasses in the bottom ring. Soon all ten glasses were full, and Molly had poured water into only one glass!

---

1. **Which of these things happened first?**

   (A) Molly said that she could fill ten glasses.

   (B) Molly poured water into the top glass.

   (C) Molly put six glasses in a circle.

2. **What did Molly do after the top glass was full?**

   (A) She set up the glasses in a special way.

   (B) She made a middle ring with three glasses.

   (C) She kept right on pouring the water.

It had been snowing for two days. It was snowing too hard to go out. Christopher was tired of staying indoors. He loved the woods in the snow, and he wanted to be outside. The next day, when Christopher woke up, the sky was clear. Christopher decided to go for a walk in the woods before breakfast. First, he put on his boots and winter coat. Then he hurried out of the house and followed a path through the snowy woods. He came to an open place. A farmer had put a big block of salt in the middle of the open place.

Next, Christopher sat down on a log. He stayed very quiet. He could see his breath making little clouds in the cold air. Soon a deer came from behind some trees and walked toward the block of salt. The deer licked the salt. Christopher held his breath while he watched. Then a branch fell off a tree and made a noise. The deer looked up. It saw Christopher and ran away.

---

1. **Which of these things happened last?**

   (A) A deer came from behind some trees.

   (B) The deer saw Christopher and ran away.

   (C) A branch fell off a tree and made a noise.

2. **What did Christopher do right after he put on his boots and winter coat?**

   (A) He sat down on a log.

   (B) He hurried out of the house.

   (C) He followed a path through the woods.

UNIT 27
A New Bat for Maria

Spring had come. For Maria and her friends, spring meant one thing—baseball! Maria would be playing ball down at the park every day after school. This year she hoped to hit her first home run.

Maria wanted to buy a new baseball bat. First, she walked to Lou's Super Store. "I'm looking for just the right baseball bat," she told Lou.

Lou thought for a minute. He walked to the back of the store and looked all around. Then Lou reached inside a box and pulled out a big bat. "Try this one," he said.

Maria took the bat and a baseball outside. First, she threw the ball into the air. Then she swung her bat. Crack! The ball flew up high. It sailed over the huge sign that said, "LOU'S SUPER STORE." Then the ball landed on the grass far away. Maria ran inside the store. "I'll take the bat!" she told Lou.

---

1. **Which of these things happened first?**

   (A) Maria took a bat and a baseball outside.

   (B) Lou reached inside a box.

   (C) Maria walked to Lou's Super Store.

2. **What happened just before the ball landed on the grass?**

   (A) The ball sailed over a huge sign.

   (B) Spring had come.

   (C) Maria ran inside the store.

UNIT 28
A Donkey Suit for Two

Meg and Greg were invited to a party. They were supposed to dress up as animals. "Let's be a donkey! I'll be the front end. You can be the back legs," Greg said.

Meg liked her brother's idea. The children told their mother about their plan. She helped them make a donkey suit.

Finally, it was time for the party. First, Greg climbed into the front part of the donkey suit. Then Meg climbed into the back part. She had to bend over when she walked. It wasn't easy! She couldn't see where she was going. "Let's go!" Greg cried. While he walked to the left, Meg walked to the right. The donkey suit began to stretch. "Stop!" Meg shouted. Then both children fell down and laughed. "I think we should have practiced walking in this suit before today!" said Meg.

---

1. **Which of these things happened last?**

    (A) Meg and Greg were invited to a party.

    (B) Meg shouted, "Stop!"

    (C) Meg and Greg fell down and laughed.

2. **What happened while Meg walked to the right?**

    (A) Greg walked to the left.

    (B) "Let's go!" Greg cried.

    (C) Greg climbed into the front part of the suit.

Hannah woke up early Saturday morning. Today was market day! She pulled on her clothes quickly. Then she ran to the kitchen. Grandfather was fixing breakfast. Hannah sat down and ate with him. Then she and Grandfather got out their baskets. They walked four blocks to the outdoor market.

"I need some round red apples," Grandfather told Hannah. "Would you go find them while I look for carrots?"

Hannah walked past two fruit stands. She looked carefully at everyone's apples. Finally, she stopped at Mrs. Bell's stand. Hannah picked out ten perfect apples. After she bought them, Hannah put the apples into her basket. Then she ran off to find Grandfather.

When Hannah showed Grandfather the apples, he looked pleased. "You always choose the best," he told her. Hannah smiled proudly.

---

1. **Which of these things happened first?**

   (A) Grandfather ate breakfast.

   (B) Hannah ran to the kitchen.

   (C) Hannah woke up early.

2. **What did Hannah do first after she bought the apples?**

   (A) She put the apples into her basket.

   (B) She stopped at Mrs. Bell's fruit stand.

   (C) She showed the apples to Grandfather.

UNIT 30
A Wish Come True

Ling had moved to a new city. He was feeling lonely. So far, he had not met any boys or girls his age. Ling went to the park and he sat on a bench for a while. Then he walked to the wishing well. Ling threw a penny into the well. "I wish I had a special friend," he said to himself.

After he made his wish, Ling stretched out on the grass. Soon he fell asleep.

When Ling woke up, a boy was standing near him. "My name is Harold," he said. "You must be new around here. Would you like to play tag?"

Ling nodded happily. He and Harold played tag with some other children. Then they made up stories about princes and dragons. Ling and Harold agreed to meet again the next day. Then each boy went home.

---

1. **Which of these things happened last?**

    (A) Ling and Harold went home.

    (B) They agreed to meet again the next day.

    (C) Ling went to the park.

2. **What did Ling do just before he fell asleep?**

    (A) He sat on a bench.

    (B) He played tag with some other children.

    (C) He stretched out on the grass.

"It's time for you to go over to Mrs. Fry's apartment now," said Mona's father. "How do you feel about taking your first piano lesson?"

"I'm not sure," said Mona. Mona walked to Mrs. Fry's apartment. Then she knocked on the door. Mrs. Fry smiled at Mona and let her in. Mona saw the piano in the corner of the room. It looked huge!

"Don't be scared," Mrs. Fry said. "Playing the piano is like tickling your toes. It's fun!"

Mona sat on the piano bench while Mrs. Fry got out some music. Mona looked at the white and black keys. Then she touched one of them. It made a pretty sound. Suddenly, she didn't feel scared anymore.

---

1. **Which of these things happened first?**

    (A) Mona walked to Mrs. Fry's apartment.

    (B) Mona had her first piano lesson.

    (C) Mrs. Fry smiled at Mona.

2. **What did Mona do while Mrs. Fry got out some music?**

    (A) She saw the piano in the corner of the room.

    (B) She sat on the piano bench.

    (C) She touched one of the piano keys.

UNIT 32
A Day at the Beach

Jesse's family went to the ocean. They had never been away from the city before. Everything was new and interesting to them.

First, Jesse and his family went swimming. Jesse loved the smell of the salt water. It was fun to ride the big waves toward the sandy beach. Jesse laughed as the waves pushed against him. It was hard to stand up!

After swimming, Jesse's family gathered shells on the beach. Then they went for a ride in a boat. The boat had a glass bottom.

Jesse looked through the bottom of the boat. He saw many different kinds of fish. Jesse's father took pictures while the captain of the boat talked. Finally, the boat stopped at the beach. Jesse and his family got off the boat. It had been a wonderful day.

---

1. **Which of these things happened last?**

   (A) The boat stopped at the beach.

   (B) Jesse's family went to the ocean.

   (C) Jesse and his family got off the boat.

2. **What happened while Jesse's father took pictures?**

   (A) The captain of the boat talked.

   (B) Jesse laughed as the waves pushed against him.

   (C) The family gathered shells.

UNIT 33
Police Dog

Three police officers saw an open window in a building. They thought someone might be in there. They knew it would take them a long time to look for the person, though. They thought a dog could find the person much faster. Dogs can use their sense of smell to find people quickly. Because of this, the officers sent for a police dog.

First, the officer with the dog took it to the window. Then he gave the dog the signal to go in and look. The dog just sat there. Next, the officer asked the other police officers to clap their hands. After they stopped clapping, he gave the dog the signal again. This time, the dog went right through the open window!

The officer turned to the others. "This dog has been visiting a lot of schools with police officers," he told them. "The dog shows the children what it can do. They all clap at what it does. So now it won't do anything until people clap for it!"

---

1. **Which of these things happened first?**

    (A) The officer took the dog to the window.

    (B) The officers saw an open window.

    (C) The officers sent for a dog to help them.

2. **What happened after the police officers started clapping?**

    (A) The dog just sat there.

    (B) The dog visited schools with them.

    (C) The dog went through the open window.

UNIT 34
Cat Bath

Cats usually clean themselves by licking. They do not usually need a bath. But sometimes a cat does need a bath. If you have ever tried to give a cat a bath, you know what a job it can be! One day, Luis decided to give his cat a bath. He filled a small tub with water. Next, he put in some soap. Then Luis searched for his cat, Tigger. He found Tigger on a chair. Luis carried the cat to the tub.

Tigger took one look at the water and gave a loud meow. Next, she jumped out of Luis' arms. She seemed to spin in the air. Then Tigger ran out of the room and hid under a bed. Luis followed her. "I'm sorry. I guess cats don't like baths," Luis said to his cat. "I guess it's lucky you know how to wash yourself." Tigger gave him an angry look. She seemed to agree.

---

1. **Which of these things happened last?**

   (A) Tigger hid under the bed.

   (B) Luis followed Tigger.

   (C) Tigger gave Luis an angry look.

2. **What did Luis do right after he put some soap in the tub?**

   (A) He searched for his cat.

   (B) He filled the tub with water.

   (C) He gave his cat a bath.

Bev sat down at her school desk. She looked at the desk next to her. Just the day before, it had been empty. Now there was a new girl sitting at the desk. Bev smiled at the new girl. "What's your name?" Bev asked.

"My name is Rajeen. I come from India," the girl said. Then the school bell rang. There was no more time to talk.

The children worked hard at their lessons. Finally, lunch time came, and Bev and Rajeen sat next to each other. Bev ate her sandwich while Rajeen talked about India. In India, Rajeen had lived in a very big city. The people there spoke in many different ways. Rajeen could speak in three different languages herself!

Bev was glad to have a new friend. She asked Rajeen to come to her house after school. Then Rajeen gave Bev a tiny wooden elephant. "This is for you, my new friend," Rajeen said.

---

1. **Which of these things happened first?**

    (A) Bev looked at the desk next to her.

    (B) Bev smiled at the new girl.

    (C) Bev sat down at her school desk.

2. **What did Bev do while Rajeen talked about India?**

    (A) She ate her sandwich.

    (B) She worked hard at her lessons.

    (C) She smiled at Rajeen.

Sam wanted to make some money, so he decided to sell rocks. First, Sam made a sign. It said, "Rocks for Sale—5 Pennies Each." Then Sam collected a big pile of rocks. He put them on a table outside. Sam sat next to the table. He waited and waited for people to buy his rocks. Nobody stopped to buy even one.

"I guess selling rocks is not a very good way to make money," he said. "But I really need the money. I need to buy a present for my dad."

Then Sam had a better idea. He got some gold paint. Next, he painted all the rocks gold. They looked very shiny. They were beautiful! Sam made a new sign that said, "Gold Rocks for Sale—1 Dollar Each." People bought every one of his gold rocks.

---

1. **Which of these things happened last?**

    (A) Sam made a new sign.

    (B) Sam painted the rocks.

    (C) People bought Sam's gold rocks.

2. **What did Sam do before he collected a pile of rocks?**

    (A) He made a sign.

    (B) He sat next to a table.

    (C) He got some gold paint.

Nina watched the rain fall outside. Then she sighed and shook her head. Nina didn't know what to do on a rainy day. She had called her friend Carla, but Carla could not come over. Nina had read a book. Then she had watched TV. Now she wanted something new to do.

At last, she thought of something. Nina took an empty jar from the kitchen. Then she measured the side of the jar. It was six inches tall. She made six marks on the side of the jar, one for every inch.

Next, Nina took the jar outside. She left it out in the rain. The rain fell harder and harder. Nina watched the rain running down the window. She watched the rain falling into her jar. When it finally stopped raining, she brought the jar inside. Nina looked at how many inches of water were in the jar. It had rained three inches that afternoon!

---

1. **Which of these things happened first?**

    (A) Nina took an empty jar from the kitchen.

    (B) It stopped raining.

    (C) Nina took the jar outside.

2. **What did Nina do after she brought the jar inside?**

    (A) She made six marks on the side of the jar.

    (B) She looked at how many inches of water were in it.

    (C) She measured the side of the jar.

Simon the Snake lived at the city zoo. Simon was a very big snake, and people loved to go to see him. Most people were glad that the big snake was behind glass, though!

One Saturday, Simon the Snake got away from the zoo. It happened when a zoo worker came into Simon's cage to feed him. While the zoo man was opening the door, Simon slid out. "Stop!" the worker shouted. Simon just kept sliding along. He slipped into the bushes.

After a few minutes, Simon came out of hiding. Nobody was around! The big snake headed for the street. Then the zoo man saw Simon. He called to a woman who worked at the zoo. They both ran toward the big snake. Simon stopped and curled up. The snake looked very much like a garden hose. "You can't fool us," the woman from the zoo said. She laughed. Then she put a big net over Simon. Soon Simon was back in the zoo.

---

1. **Which of these things happened last?**

    (A) Simon stopped and curled up.

    (B) The woman from the zoo laughed.

    (C) The woman put a net over Simon.

2. **What happened while the zoo man opened the door of Simon's cage?**

    (A) Simon slid out.

    (B) The man shouted, "Stop!"

    (C) Simon slipped into the bushes.

In Unit 34, you read about a boy who tried to give his cat a bath. He didn't have much luck. Giving a dog a bath, though, is something many people do.

Think about the steps you would follow to give a dog a bath. If you have no dog, imagine what to do. What things would you need for the bath? What would you do first? What would you do last?

A. Exercising Your Skill

Look at the headings below. Write the headings on paper. Then write words that belong under each heading.

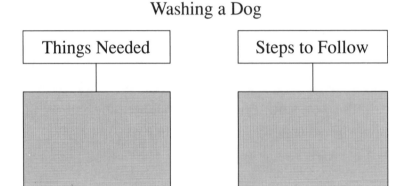

Washing a Dog

| Things Needed | Steps to Follow |

B. Expanding Your Skill

For each step in washing a dog, something can go wrong. For example, suppose you pour water over the dog. The dog might shake water all over you! Pick two steps to follow in washing a dog. For each step, tell something that could go wrong after you follow the step.

C. Exploring Language

Pick an animal from the box. Write directions on how to give that animal a bath. Make up what you don't know. Be sure to give your directions in first-to-last order.

turtle	pig	giraffe
elephant	horse	alligator

D. Expressing Yourself

Do one of these things.

1. Suppose you are a dog. Someone is giving you a bath. How would you describe what is happening? What does the bath feel like? Do you like it or hate it? Write a story as if a dog is telling about its bath.

2. Think about the steps you follow when you eat breakfast. Then act them out in front of your class, in order. Ask people to guess what each step is.

3. Look at the story for Unit 34. What things happened in the story? Draw pictures of three important things that happened. Use three pieces of paper. On the bottom of each drawing, write what is happening in the picture. Put the pictures in first-to-last order.

Ian liked to collect pennies. He had lots of shiny new pennies and a few old ones.

He kept the pennies in a jar in his room. One day Ian's grandmother came for a visit. She gave Ian a big jar of her pennies. "I collected these pennies when I was little," she told Ian.

Grandmother and Ian brought the jar into the living room. After they turned the jar over, they spread the pennies out on the floor. Then Ian looked at the coins carefully. He looked to see when each coin was made. Some of them were 100 years old!

After he had looked at each coin, Ian put the pennies in a safe place. He hoped he could give them to his own children someday.

---

1. **Which of these things happened first?**

   (A) Ian put his grandmother's pennies in a safe place.

   (B) Ian's grandmother came for a visit.

   (C) Ian looked at some very old pennies.

2. **What happened right after Grandmother and Ian turned the jar over?**

   (A) They spread the pennies out on the floor.

   (B) Ian found some shiny new pennies.

   (C) They brought the jar into the living room.

Wendy and her brother Tim walked to the library. They pulled an empty red wagon behind them. When they got to the library, Wendy and Tim left the wagon outside. They walked into the library. Wendy found eight books to read. Tim found ten books to read. Next, they piled their books on the front desk.

"Goodness!" said the woman at the desk. "How will you carry all those books?"

"Don't worry," said Tim.

"How will you read all those books?" the woman asked.

"Don't worry," said Wendy.

Tim and Wendy carried their books out to the red wagon. They put the books in the wagon and pulled it home. Then they began to read and read and read.

---

1. **Which of these things happened last?**

   (A) Tim and Wendy put their books in the wagon.

   (B) Tim and Wendy read their library books.

   (C) Tim and Wendy walked to the library.

2. **What happened just before Wendy found eight books to read?**

   (A) The woman at the desk said, "Goodness!"

   (B) Tim found ten books to read.

   (C) Wendy and Tim walked into the library.

Have you ever heard the story of the person who made the first United States flag? She made it even before the country had its name. The king of England still ruled the country.

Many people did not want the king to be in charge, though. They wanted to be a free country. That is why George Washington and two other men went to see Betsy Ross one day in the year 1776. They were going to fight for a free country, and they wanted that country to have a flag.

Betsy Ross was known for her fine work with cloth. She was the right person to make a special flag. First, she and the three men talked about what kind of flag it should be. Then Betsy Ross set to work on the idea. She used three colors of cloth—red, white, and blue. She made red and white stripes. Next, she put white stars on blue cloth. Finally, she put all the parts together. Everyone agreed that the flag she had made was just right for the new country.

---

1. **Which of these things happened first?**

   (A) Betsy Ross made red and white stripes.

   (B) George Washington went to see Betsy Ross.

   (C) Everyone agreed that the flag was just right.

2. **What did Betsy Ross do after she put white stars on blue cloth?**

   (A) She made red and white stripes.

   (B) She talked with the three men.

   (C) She put all the parts together.

UNIT 42
A Day in the City

Carlos and his father decided to spend a day in the city. They woke up early and got on a train. As the train came nearer and nearer to the city, they saw more and more buildings. When they were almost in the middle of the city, the train went under the ground. Then it came to a stop.

Carlos and his father got out of the train and climbed up some stairs. Soon they were on a busy street. They walked for many blocks. Carlos saw hundreds of buses, cars, and people. Everybody seemed to be in a hurry. Next, Carlos and his father bought lunch and ate it in a park. Carlos fed the birds some of his bread.

After they finished lunch, Carlos and his father went inside a tall building. They rode an elevator to the top. Carlos looked out a window there. Everything in the big city suddenly looked small.

---

1. **Which of these things happened last?**

   (A) Carlos and his father rode in an elevator.

   (B) Carlos looked out a window in the tall building.

   (C) Carlos and his father got out of the train.

2. **What did Carlos and his father do before they bought lunch?**

   (A) They fed the birds some bread.

   (B) They walked for many blocks.

   (C) They went inside a tall building.

Here's how to make a small indoor garden.

First, gather together what you need. Find a large glass bowl. Next, get some small plants that need very little water to grow. Then gather some dirt for planting. Finally, get some small stones and some water. Ask someone to help if you can't find everything you need.

Put the small stones on the bottom of the bowl. On top of the stones, put about one and a half inches of dirt. Then plant the small plants in the dirt. Put a little water in your garden. You can add more water when the dirt looks dry.

Place the bowl where it can be seen and will get some sunlight. Make sure it isn't in a very hot or very cold place.

---

1. **Which of these things should you do first?**

    (A) Put water in the bowl.

    (B) Put small stones in the bowl.

    (C) Gather the things you need.

2. **What should you do after you put dirt in the bowl?**

    (A) Put the bowl in some sunlight.

    (B) Plant the small plants.

    (C) Put the stones in the bowl.

Dee and her brother Zeke like to play tricks on each other on April Fool's Day. They like to see who can get the last laugh.

Last year, Dee planned a special joke. She got up early on April Fool's Day. She tiptoed into her brother's room. Zeke was sleeping soundly. Dee picked up Zeke's clock. She changed the time from seven o'clock to eight o'clock. She set the clock back down on the table very quietly. Then she went back to the door and turned on the light. "Time to get up!" she shouted. "You're late for school!"

Zeke sat up in bed. He didn't look surprised. In fact, he was smiling. Then he laughed. "I knew you would change the clock," Zeke said. "I changed yours first. Did you know it's only six o'clock?" Zeke went back to sleep. He had had the last laugh!

---

1. **Which of these things happened last?**

   (A) Zeke sat up in bed.

   (B) Dee tiptoed into Zeke's room.

   (C) Dee changed the time on Zeke's clock.

2. **What happened before Dee turned on Zeke's light?**

   (A) Zeke laughed.

   (B) Dee changed the time on Zeke's clock.

   (C) Dee shouted, "Time to get up!"

Something Wonderful

Jason decided to dig in his backyard. Maybe some gold was hidden there! First, Jason talked to his mother about it. "May I dig in the yard?" he asked.

"You may dig in the flower bed," his mother said. "But please don't dig up the grass. Tell me if you find something wonderful!"

Jason dug a small hole in the garden. He found two worms. He put them into an old can with some dirt. Maybe they would come in handy sometime. Then he found a bottle cap and put it into his pocket. Next, Jason found a rock. As he dug around the rock, Jason came across an old silver spoon. "Wow! This is almost as good as finding gold," Jason said. He put the spoon into his pocket. Then he put the dirt back in place.

---

1. **Which of these things happened first?**

   (A) Jason dug in his backyard.

   (B) Jason put the dirt back in place.

   (C) Jason talked to his mother.

2. **What happened as Jason dug around the rock?**

   (A) He found a bottle cap.

   (B) He came across a spoon.

   (C) He found two worms.

UNIT 46
Potato Stories

Kiki's father wanted to make potato soup. He asked Kiki to get some potatoes for him. Kiki looked in the potato bag. She pulled out a big potato. Then Kiki laughed. The potato looked like a person's head! It had two "eyes" and a bump for a nose. "This potato is too funny to use," she said. Kiki put it back into the bag.

Kiki looked for another potato. She pulled out a small one. This one looked like a shoe! "This potato is too cute to use," she said.

Next, Kiki found a potato that looked like a duck and one that looked like a large peanut shell. Kiki kept pulling out potatoes and making up stories about them.

"I give up," Kiki's father said at last. He made bean soup instead.

---

1. **Which of these things happened last?**

   (A) Kiki's father said, "I give up."

   (B) Kiki looked for a potato.

   (C) Kiki's father made bean soup.

2. **What happened right after Kiki pulled out a big potato?**

   (A) She laughed.

   (B) Her father made bean soup.

   (C) She found a potato that looked like a duck.

UNIT 47
The Slow Race

Levar and Toby were good friends. They were the same age, and they liked to do all the same things. They played ball together, they went swimming together, and they ate lunch together at school. Most of all, they loved to race each other. They held running races, crawling races, and jumping races.

One day, Toby and Levar held a race to see who was slowest! First Levar and Toby lined up on the sidewalk. Then Toby called, "Go!" Next, Levar moved forward one step. Toby moved forward half a step. While Toby stood still, Levar moved back a step.

"This isn't very much fun," Toby said.

"You're right," Levar agreed.

The boys decided that the slow race was a tie. Then they held a hopping race.

---

1. **Which of these things happened first?**

    (A) Toby called, "Go!"

    (B) Levar and Toby lined up on the sidewalk.

    (C) The boys decided to hold a hopping race.

2. **What did Levar do while Toby stood still?**

    (A) Levar moved forward one step.

    (B) Levar decided the race was a tie.

    (C) Levar moved back a step.

Fran's family was moving to a new home. The days before moving were very busy. Fran and her family had to pack all their things into boxes. Then, on moving day, they all helped carry the boxes to the big moving van. Everything from the house had to go on the van.

Fran felt happy about moving to a new house. She also felt sad about leaving her old house. Before Fran left, she said good-by to the house. First, she walked into her old room. "Good-by, room!" she said. Next, she looked into every room upstairs. The rooms looked cold and bare. Then she went downstairs. She walked from one empty room to another. "Good-by, downstairs!" Fran said.

Then Fran walked to the front porch. She reached into her pocket for her lucky penny. Fran put the penny under the porch steps. "Someday I'll come back for this penny," she said. Then she ran to the moving van.

---

1. **Which of these things happened last?**

    (A) Fran's family carried boxes to the moving van.

    (B) Fran ran to the moving van.

    (C) Fran put a penny under the porch.

2. **What did Fran do just before she reached into her pocket for her lucky penny?**

    (A) She walked to the front porch.

    (B) She said she'd come back for the penny someday.

    (C) She packed her things into boxes.

Vincent wanted to learn about the stars. First, he got a book about stars from the library. The book showed a map of the stars. Vincent looked carefully at the map. Many of the stars had names. Sometimes a set of stars in one part of the sky seemed to make a picture. These star pictures also had names.

One night Vincent went outside to see the stars for himself. He stretched out on the grass and looked up at the clear sky.

"I will try to find the North Star," Vincent said. First he had to find a set of stars called the Big Dipper. Two stars in the Big Dipper would point toward the North Star. Vincent found the Big Dipper. Next, he looked for the North Star. There it was! Then Vincent looked for some other special stars. Suddenly, he saw a shooting star. It was like a small light falling to the earth.

---

1. **Which of these things happened first?**

    (A) Vincent looked at a map of the stars.

    (B) Vincent got a book about stars from the library.

    (C) Vincent looked for the North Star.

2. **What did Vincent do just after he went outside one night?**

    (A) He stretched out on the grass.

    (B) He saw a shooting star.

    (C) He looked at a map of the stars.

UNIT 50
Learning to Roller-Skate

Have you ever tried roller-skating? It can be a lot of fun. It may be hard to get started, though.

First, you need to get some skates that fit. Then you need to find a smooth, safe place to skate. On your first day of skating, be sure to wear old clothes that cover your knees. You may fall down a few times.

After you put on your skates, you are ready to begin skating—almost. First, you must stand up on the skates! Hold onto a friend or a fence, and stand up slowly. Keep holding on until you feel safe. Next, push off with one skate. Lift your other foot so that you are rolling on just one skate. As you begin to slow down, put your other foot down and push off with the foot that has been rolling along. Now you are rolling on the other skate. Keep pushing off and rolling, first with one foot, then with the other. Don't bend over or look down at your skates. Soon you will be skating along smoothly.

---

1. **Which of these things do you do first?**

   (A) You push off with one skate.

   (B) You begin to slow down.

   (C) You stand up slowly.

2. **What do you do before you put on the skates?**

   (A) You lift one foot then the other.

   (B) You find a safe place to skate.

   (C) You hold on until you feel safe.

In Unit 50, you read about roller-skating. Roller skates can make a fun birthday present. Someone might pick them out for you someday.

What kind of birthday present would you buy or make for a friend? How would you pick it? Would you put it in a box? Would you put paper around it? (To put paper around it is to *wrap* it.) Think about the steps you follow to give a birthday present.

A. Exercising Your Skill

Look at the headings below. Write the headings on a paper. Then write words that belong under each heading.

Giving a Birthday Present

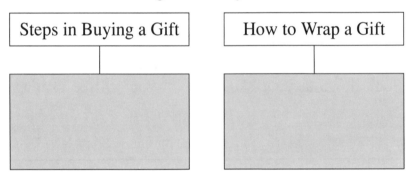

Steps in Buying a Gift	How to Wrap a Gift

B. Expanding Your Skill

Giving a birthday present is fun. Getting a birthday present may be even more fun. What do you do after someone gives you a present? Write three things that you do. List them in first-to-last order.

C. Exploring Language

Pretend that today is your birthday. There are three boxes for you to open. One is as tall as you are. Another box is nearly as tiny as a mouse. The third box is in between the size of the other two.

Which box will you open first? Which box will you open last? Write a story about opening the boxes. Tell what order you open them in. Name what is inside each box.

D. Expressing Yourself

Do one of these things.

1. Look at the story for Unit 50. Think about learning to roller-skate. If you wanted to learn, what would you have to do? Write three sentences that tell what you would do.

2. Play a game called "What's-in-the-Box?" First choose something small to put into a box. It could be a toy, a pen, a coin, or anything else you wish. Next put the thing into a box. Then give the box to a friend. Let your friend shake the box. Then give your friend ten chances to guess what is inside.

3. Make a birthday wish list. Think about what you want most for your birthday. Put that at the top of your list. Write the other things you want in order below the thing you want most.